Christine Caine & Lisa Harper

The Promise and Power of Easter

Captivated by the Cross and Resurrection of Jesus

HarperChristian Resources

Contents

Welcome
From Christine and Lisa

The resurrection of Jesus Christ stands as the most pivotal event in human history. On Easter, we rejoice in Jesus' triumph over the grave, His victory over death forever. In the early centuries of Christianity, believers set aside a time for fasting, prayer, and reflection, which eventually became known as Lent.

Considering the weeks leading up to Easter are crucial, we do ourselves a disservice by thinking of Easter as merely a single day on the calendar. As author and speaker Barbara Johnson of Women of Faith famously said, "We are Easter people living in a Good Friday world." This perspective reminds us to live in the joy and hope of the resurrection every day.

Easter is so much more than a 24-hour period; it forms the metanarrative for us as followers of Christ. So, in this study, we're not only preparing our hearts for the resurrection, but we are also going to get a bigger picture of the Easter people we are called to be.

What we have discovered is that as we focus on the promise and power of Jesus' death and resurrection, we have the opportunity to draw closer to Christ and remove every obstacle that gets in the way. Through what Jesus did on the cross, we find new life in Christ. We discover purpose and see opportunities to share this new life everywhere we go, with everyone, in every way.

As we embark on this Easter journey, may you find yourself awakening to Jesus anew—through the details of His life, the agony of His death, and the overwhelming joy of His resurrection.

Chris   Lisa

How to Use This Guide

OVERVIEW

The Promise and Power of Easter Bible study is divided into four sessions. Every session includes Video Teaching Notes, Group Discussion, Call to Action, Closing Prayer, and Between Sessions Personal Bible Study. As a group, you will watch the video and then use the video notes and questions to engage in active conversation. The goal is to develop genuine relationships and to be fully equipped to share the good news of God's redemption of us through His son, Jesus.

GROUP SIZE

This four-session video Bible study is designed to be experienced in a group setting such as a Bible study, Sunday school class, retreat, small-group, or online gathering. If your gathering is large, you may want to consider splitting everyone into smaller groups of five to eight people. This will ensure that everyone has an opportunity to participate in the discussions.

MATERIALS NEEDED

Everyone in your group will need a copy of this study guide, which includes personal streaming video access, notes for the video teachings, discussion questions, and personal Bible studies in between group meetings. A leader's guide—including best practices—is found at the back of each study guide.

FACILITATION

Depending on how your group is formatted, you may need to appoint a person to serve as a facilitator. This person will be responsible for starting the video and keeping track of time during discussions. Facilitators should be prepared to read the discussion questions aloud, monitor discussions, encourage everyone in the group to engage, and ensure that everyone has the opportunity to participate.

PERSONAL STUDIES

Between group meetings, maximize the impact of this study on Easter by working through the personal Bible study section. Treat each personal Bible study like committed time with the Lord and your Bible in whatever way works best for your schedule. Allowing time across multiple days provides the greatest opportunity for marinating in God's Word, as well as for letting the teaching sink in and take root. These personal studies are not intended to be burdensome or time-consuming, but to help you apply the lessons learned to your everyday, personal life for growth and connection.

STATIONS OF THE CROSS

Traditionally a Catholic tracing of the last moments of Jesus' life, we have included a visual telling of Jesus' last days through His resurrection. We hope this helps you trace this incredible story in a simple and beautiful way. We encourage you to look up each Scripture reference as you use this tool.

SCRIPTURE CUTOUT ARTWORK

We have selected four specific verses from the Bible that carry the Easter narrative as we can experience it today. Each verse page is designed to be cut out and will fit in a standard 8x10 matte frame. Our hope is that you will be reminded of the promise and power of Easter and continue to live captivated by the cross and resurrection of Jesus every day!

"From the very beginning God said, 'You're worth so much to Me that I will send My Son, and He will die to reconcile you to Myself.' That's Easter."

LISA HARPER

God's Redemptive Plan for the World

Video

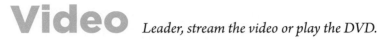

Leader, stream the video or play the DVD.

Each video opens with a short introduction vignette, followed by the teaching session. **As you watch, take notes on anything that stands out to you.**

SCRIPTURE: Luke 24:25–26; Genesis 12:2–20; Genesis 15

Story of running

Our trinitarian God is restoring us

Road to Emmaus

Abraham

I will bless you

Blood covenant

VOCABULARY	DEFINITION
HERMENEUTIC	the lens through which we look at God and His Word
THEOPHANY	the physical representation of God Himself
LAW of FIRST MENTION	when something happens repeatedly in Scripture, pay attention to the details of the first occurrence
EXEGESIS	to draw knowledge out of something

Group Discussion

1. **Think about your personal experience with Easter and the weeks leading up to the event.**

   • Did you celebrate either or both Easter and Lent as a child?

   • Do you celebrate either today? How so?

   • What is your understanding of the season?

   "I think the common perception is to think of the God of the Old Testament as a punitive God of wrath and the God of the New Testament as a Jesus kind of grace. Yet God the Father, God the Son, and God the Holy Spirit are perfectly eternal, and that posture of redeeming us traces all the way to the very beginning."

2. **Discuss the following.**

   • Do you ever think of the God of the Old Testament as different from the God of the New Testament? How so?

   • Why is it important to remember that the Father, Jesus, and the Holy Spirit have existed in unison since the beginning?

3. **Invite a few volunteers to read Luke 24:13–27, and then respond to the following questions.**

   • Why were those on the road to Emmaus so confused by recent events?

   • How does Jesus respond to them?

- Why does Jesus turn to Moses and all the prophets to reveal Himself?

- Why is it important to study Moses and the prophets to learn more about Jesus?

"If you go back to the beginning of the story of God in Genesis, you'll find the red thread of redemption has always been there."

4. **Invite a few volunteers to read Genesis 15, and then respond to the following questions.**

   - What promise was Abraham waiting for God to fulfill?

   - How does God assure Abraham He will fulfill this promise?

   - Why does God institute a binding blood covenant? What is different about this covenant?

   - What does this reveal about God's commitment to fulfill His promises?

5. **Consider how the blood covenant points to Easter and Christ's sacrifice on the cross.**

   - What changes in your understanding of just how precise, deliberate, and intentional God is with every move from the Old Testament to the New?

- What does God's willingness to fulfill His promises—even when we break ours—reveal about God's character? His love? His commitment to us?

- In what ways do you struggle to see yourself the way God sees you—as the object of His affection?

- Where do you most need your heart awakened to Jesus' power and presence this Easter season?

"It's a huge deal that the smoking fire pot and flaming torch represent God Himself—the Creator, Redeemer, and King of kings—walking through the blood. He knows the covenant will be broken because of sin, but He will pay the price in His blood on Easter. This didn't start in the New Testament—it started in Genesis. That's why Easter is not just a point in history. It's the point of history. We have always been and will always be the objects of His affection."

Call to Action

Leader, you will need some pieces of paper, about a quarter- or half-page for this exercise.

Pass out a piece of paper to each group member. Invite each person to write down something she is seeking restoration or resolve for this Easter season. Place each slip of paper into a bowl or basket, mix them up, then have each person draw one. Pray over that restoration for the next four weeks.

Closing Prayer

Select a volunteer to read the closing prayer over the group.

Lord, Your love for us is amazing and traces back to before the beginning of time. For thousands of years, You have been planning to come in human form and redeem us. We are so grateful. We ask that Your resurrection would be alive in our hearts—the reality of who You are, all You've done, and all You've called us to become. We love You. In Jesus' name. Amen.

Personal Study

This section is created as a guide to
personally study and further explore God's
Word in anticipation of our Savior's sacrifice.

Don't forget to pray for personal restoration
or resolve for one of your fellow group
members throughout this week.

• • •

LESSON ONE

The season leading up to Easter invites us to reflect on our lives and relationship with Jesus and enter a time of preparation for the death and resurrection of Christ.

What's one meaningful way you've prepared your heart for Easter in the past?

In Italy, the seven weeks leading up to Easter, known as Lent, are rich with traditions. This period begins on Ash Wednesday, when the faithful receive ashes on their foreheads as a symbol of repentance. Many Italians observe Lent by giving up certain foods or habits, focusing on prayer, fasting, and doing acts of charity. In one province, seven dolls dressed in black are placed in a public location. One disappears every Sunday as a kind of countdown to Easter. Holy Week, the final days before Easter, holds special significance with processions and reenactments of Jesus' suffering, known as the Passion of Christ. The week culminates in the joyous celebration of Easter.

In Greece, Lent is known as "Great Lent" and begins with "Clean Monday," a day filled with outdoor activities, in particular kite flying, which symbolizes "trying to reach the divine" and the cleansing of sins. Greeks adhere to a diet during the weeks leading up to Easter, in order to simplify their diet and focus intentionally on spiritual matters. Orthodox Greeks avoid meat and all their byproducts including cheese, milk, and eggs, as well as oil and wine. Religious services are held on Fridays. Holy Week features nightly church services, culminating in a procession on Good Friday and special service at midnight on Holy Saturday. In celebration of Easter, eggs are dyed red to symbolize the blood of Jesus and renewed life. The resurrection is celebrated with candles, fireworks, and a feast with family and friends.

In Ethiopia, Lent is observed by the Ethiopian Orthodox Church for fifteen days longer than the traditional forty-day period with a rigorous fast. The weeks leading up to Easter are marked by increased prayer, church attendance, and giving. Services are held daily, with a focus on repentance and spiritual renewal. Holy Week features special liturgies and the "Procession of the Cross," which features a large, ornate cross. On Good Friday, many attend church services and engage in acts of penance. Easter Sunday is celebrated with a festive meal, breaking the fast with dishes like spicy chicken stew.

All these practices help participants engage in a hope-filled anticipation, preparation, and celebration of Christ's resurrection.

🌿 Which of these practices intrigues you the most? Why?

🌿 Which of these practices (or others) might help you engage more intentionally as you prepare for Jesus' resurrection?

In this season of Easter, where do you most need to encounter Jesus in your life? Circle all that apply.

Healing in relationships   Overcoming addiction

Finding purpose   Building connections

Overcoming fear   Decision making

Extending forgiveness   Finding peace

Seeking healing   Knowing my identity in Christ

Wisdom in parenting   Strengthening my relationship with God

Creating balance   Other: _____

Grieving fully

Where do you most need to experience the healing power and presence of Jesus?

In the space below, write a prayer that exchanges hurt for forgiveness and healing, fear for faith, and hesitations for trust. Then ask Jesus to fill you with hope-filled anticipation for how He might meet and renew you during Easter.

• • •

LESSON TWO

The story of Adam and Eve in Genesis 3 is foundational for understanding our need for Jesus, and it helps set the stage for the celebration of His long-awaited birth. In this important chapter of the Bible, the serpent tempts Eve to eat from the tree of the knowledge of good and evil, which God had forbidden. The serpent's cunning questions sow doubt into Eve and lead her to disobey God's command. She takes some of the fruit and eats it, and then gives some to Adam, who also eats it.

Read Genesis 3:1–6.

🌿 How does the serpent's question to Eve challenge her understanding of God's command?

🌿 What motivates Eve to eat the forbidden fruit, and how does this reflect our human tendencies?

Once Adam and Eve disobey God, everything changes, including the way they see each other and the world.

Read Genesis 3:7–13.

🌿 How do Adam and Eve respond to each other? To God?

🌿 What is the impact of disobedience to God, also known as sin, on their relationships?

God pronounces judgments because of their disobedience: the serpent is cursed, and hostility is placed between the serpent and the woman's offspring. Eve will experience pain in childbirth, and Adam will work hard for food from difficult ground. They are then expelled from the garden to prevent them from eating from the tree of life and living forever in their sinful state. Yet, even with their disobedience, God lays the blueprint for the salvation of humanity.

Genesis 3:15 is sometimes referred to as the "protoevangelium," or "first gospel," because it contains the first of God's plan for salvation through Jesus Christ. In the aftermath of Adam and Eve's disobedience, this verse provides hope and a promise of redemption.

In the space below, write Genesis 3:15.

In this verse, God addresses the serpent (Satan) after the disobedience of the original couple. Several elements of this passage point to Jesus and the plan of salvation for humanity.

The "enmity" or hostility between the serpent and the woman are representative of the ongoing conflict, represented by the serpent, or Satan, and humanity.

The "offspring" or "seed" refers to the descendants of Eve, but ultimately points to one specific descendant: Jesus.

The "crushing" of the serpent's head foreshadows the ultimate defeat of Satan and the power of sin through Jesus' death and resurrection.

The "strike" on the heel contrasts with the "crushing" of the head. A strike on the heel can be survived, but a crushing of the head cannot. The striking can be interpreted as the suffering and crucifixion of Jesus, and Jesus' resurrection reveals His victory over death and all evil.

How does Genesis 3:15 reveal the incredible depth of God's love and His commitment to redeeming humanity?

Jesus' death and resurrection fulfill the promise of victory over death.

Read 1 Corinthians 15:55–57.

How does Paul personify death in these verses, and what is the significance of challenging death in this manner?

In what ways can understanding Jesus' victory over death impact your daily life, spiritual walk, and understanding of suffering and overcoming?

Jesus' death and resurrection make it possible to walk in relationship with God.

Read 2 Corinthians 5:18–19.

What does it mean to be reconciled to God through Jesus, and how does this reflect the promise in Genesis 3:15?

Jesus' death and resurrection reveal that evil does not win.

Read Romans 16:20.

🌿 How does Paul's reference to God crushing Satan under our feet relate to Genesis 3:15?

Jesus' victory over death and sin provides hope and redemption for all who believe.

Read John 3:16.

🌿 What is the promise and power available to everyone because of Jesus' sacrifice?

Tucked into Genesis 3 is the promise of Jesus who will fulfill God's plan and promises. Yet it's far from the only moment in Genesis that points to Jesus as the one who will redeem humanity—as we'll discover in the next lesson of personal study.

• • •
LESSON THREE

We all have situations and circumstances that can cause us to doubt God's promises, and Abram was no exception. Abram's story begins with God commanding him to leave his homeland in Ur to go to an unfamiliar land, which would later be revealed as Canaan. God promises to make Abram into a great nation, bless him, and make his name great. By faith, Abram obeys and travels with his wife, Sarai, and his nephew, Lot, to Canaan. God appears to Abram there, and reaffirms His promise, declaring that He will give the land to Abram's descendants, but a severe drought drives Abram to Egypt (Genesis 12).

Abram and Lot return to Canaan, but their growing herds create strife, and so Abram offers Lot the first choice of the land. Lot chooses the best land for himself, and Abram is left with Canaan. Once again, God reiterates His promise to Abram (Genesis 13).

When we catch up with the aging Abram in Genesis 15, he is concerned that he and Sarai are childless. He wonders how God will make his descendants as numerous as the stars in the sky, since he doesn't have a single child. Once again, God assures Abram that his descendants will be abundant and will inherit the land. Abram believes God's promise, and his faith is credited to him as righteousness. To formalize the covenant or promise, God instructs Abram to prepare a sacrificial ritual.

Read Genesis 15:1.

   What does God instruct Abram to do?

How does God's promise to Abram foreshadow the protection and reward we find in Christ?

Despite multiple assurances from God that Abram will have many descendants, he still struggles with doubt. This highlights Abram's humanity and his inability to see beyond his current circumstances. Despite Abram's anxiety about his lack of an heir, God reassures him with a powerful promise, reinforcing the unshakeable nature of God's covenant with Abram.

Read Genesis 15:2–5 and Galatians 3:6–9, 29.

How does God's promise find its ultimate fulfillment in the spiritual descendants of Abraham through Christ?

Abram's belief, despite his uncertainties, is counted as righteousness, establishing a foundational principle for the relationship between God and His people.

Read Genesis 15:6–11.

In the space below, draw a representative picture of what's described.

Read Genesis 15:12 and Matthew 27:45–46.

How does this darkness symbolize the suffering and death that Christ would endure?

God gives Abram a broader perspective on His unfolding divine plan. The foretelling goes beyond the Israelites' enslavement in Egypt and extends to a larger divine narrative that God has been working throughout history.

Read Genesis 15:13–16 and Romans 6:17–18.

What does God say about the future slavery and freedom of Abram's descendants?

How does this prophecy parallel the slavery of sin and the freedom brought through Christ?

God ratifies the covenant to Abram through a *theophany*, a visible manifestation of God. The firepot and torch moving between the animal pieces symbolize God's binding promise to Abram. Such rituals were traditional methods of covenant-making in ancient times. By passing through the pieces, God demonstrates that He alone assumes the covenant's obligations and consequences.

Read Genesis 15:17–21 and Luke 22:20.

 How does this covenant foreshadow the new covenant made through the blood of Christ?

"God tells us that when the covenant between us is broken—and it will be because we're human and because of sin—He'll have already paid the price."

Read Hebrews 8:6.

 How does the new covenant with Christ compare with the old covenant?

How does understanding the connection between Genesis 15 and Easter deepen our appreciation for Christ's resurrection?

Genesis 15 is a foundational chapter that sets the stage for God's redemptive plan through Jesus Christ. The covenant with Abram, marked by faith, promise, and sacrifice, points forward to the ultimate fulfillment in Christ's death and resurrection. By studying this chapter, we gain a deeper understanding of God's faithfulness and the significance of Easter.

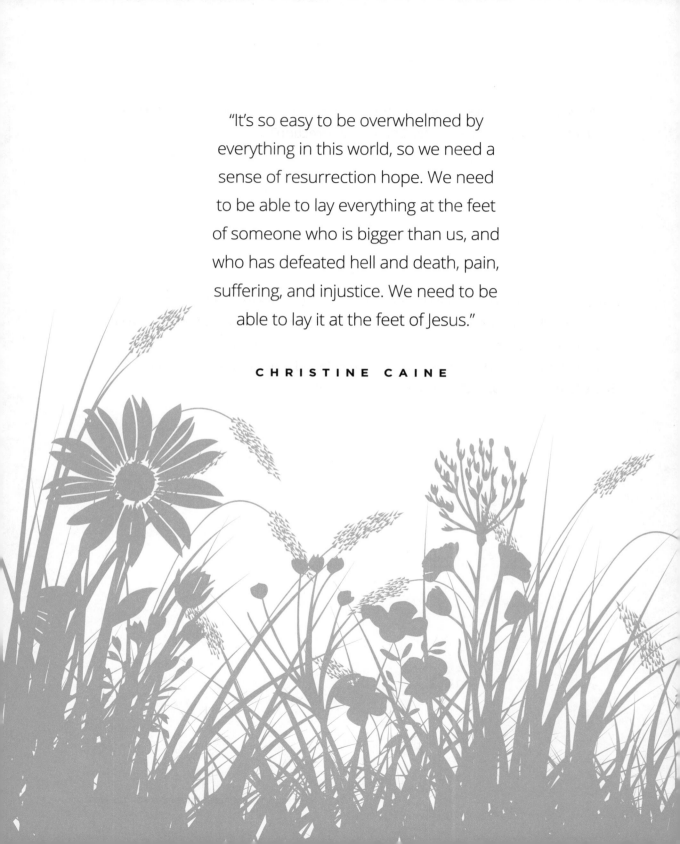

"It's so easy to be overwhelmed by everything in this world, so we need a sense of resurrection hope. We need to be able to lay everything at the feet of someone who is bigger than us, and who has defeated hell and death, pain, suffering, and injustice. We need to be able to lay it at the feet of Jesus."

CHRISTINE CAINE

Pursuing God's Presence

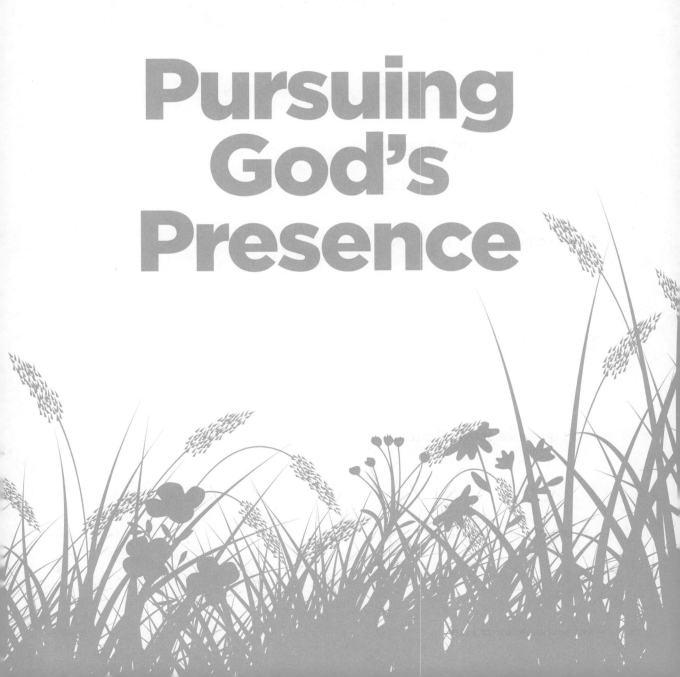

Video

Leader, stream the video or play the DVD.

Each video opens with a short introduction vignette, followed by the teaching session. **As you watch, take notes on anything that stands out to you.**

SCRIPTURE: Exodus 33

We all have things that hinder us

A spiritual chiropractic adjustment

Golden calf

Joshua lingers

God's presence above all else

Get out of the grandstands

Group Discussion

"The whole goal of our Christian life is that we become more like Jesus, and yet we can let so many things get in the way. The weeks before Easter give us the opportunity for reflection, assessment, and evaluation."

1. **Think about where you are spiritually in this Easter season.**

    • To what are you giving the largest amounts of your time, attention, and resources? (Remember: These can be good things as well as not so good things!)

    • Is there anything potentially taking precedence over God in your life?

    • What are specific ways you can focus more on the Lord in your everyday life?

    • How does being in God's presence help you realign your priorities?

2. **Even the Israelites struggled to maintain focus on the goodness of God after leaving Egypt. Invite a few volunteers to read Exodus 32:1–8, and then respond to the following questions.**

    • How do the Israelites respond to God after all he has done? (Refer to Exodus 14-17 for examples of liberation from slavery, crossing Red Sea, provision through miracles)

    • On a scale of one to ten, how quickly can you forget all that God has done for you?

    • What do the Israelites worship other than God?

3. **Consider the following.**

    - What tends to draw your attention, time, energy, and worship other than God?

    - What are three changes you could make to more fully devote yourself to God?

4. **Invite a few volunteers to read Exodus 33:7–17, and then respond to the following questions.**

    - What does Joshua learn about the character of God and the relationship between Moses and God by lingering? To *linger* is "to remain longer in a place than is required."

    - What does it look like for you to linger with God?

    - How does spending time with God affect your attitude, outlook, and response to life?

    - What differences do you notice when you don't spend time with God?

"When you linger around God, it's interesting the kind of conversations that you are going to hear."

5. **Invite two volunteers to read Deuteronomy 31:8 and Hebrews 13:5, and then respond to the following questions.**

    - What comfort does it give you to know that God never changes?

- Why is it meaningful to you that God promises to never leave you?

- If you can, describe a time when you were carrying the weight of the world on your shoulders and how time spent in the presence of God changed everything.

> *"When we don't take spiritual stock regularly, there are things we inadvertently allow into our lives that surprise us. It's like they pop up and we think, okay, where did that come from? Like when we find that our attitude is not quite what it should be. That's how we often discover the things that hinder us in our growth and development to become more Christlike."*

6. **Explore these questions.**

- How are you being tempted to sit in the grandstands and watch rather than run your race of faith?

- Where have you believed that you've made too many mistakes to be close to God?

- How is Christ challenging you to let go of everything that encumbers you to run your race of faith this Easter season?

- What changes can you make now so can you finish your race of faith well?

Call to Action

Leader, you will need some pieces of paper, about a quarter- or half-page for this exercise.

Pass out a piece of paper to each group member. Invite each person to write down an area where they need to get out of the grandstands and start running the race of faith this Easter season. Place each slip of paper into a bowl or basket, mix them up, then have each person draw one. Pray over that longing or hope for the remaining weeks.

Closing Prayer

Select a volunteer to read the closing prayer over the group.

Lord, through Your death and resurrection, You have given us full access to You. Show us the ways we've become distracted and pursued Your blessings more than Your presence. Reveal the ways we're sitting in the grandstands rather than running the race of faith before us. May we be transformed by Your presence every day. In Jesus' name. Amen.

SESSION 2

SESSION 2
Personal
Study

Don't forget to pray throughout this week for
where or how one of your fellow group members
needs to start running their race!

LESSON ONE

I (Christine) grew up in a Greek Orthodox home, so we had a forty-day period of Lent to prepare for Easter, which was really forty-six days. It wasn't forty days, because you weren't allowed to eat what you wanted for six days, but then on the seventh day, which was Sunday, you could eat anything. So naturally, the focus was on eating all that we had refrained from eating during the week.

Today, people might not give up particular foods, but refrain from social media or streaming shows to create more time to focus on Jesus—which is the point of it all. Whatever that may look like for you in length or practice, I think it's something we should consider year round, regularly assessing and evaluating where we are spiritually, and where we want to grow.

During the study times for this session, we're going to carve out time for a deeper, intentional assessment of where you are in your relationship with God, and where you might want to make some adjustments.

Reflecting on the following, how often are you engaging in each one weekly? Mark your responses.

1 = Not at all, 2 = Somewhat frequently, 3 = Often, 4 = Almost always

① — ② — ③ — ④ Talking to God and praying

① — ② — ③ — ④ Enjoying God's presence

① — ② — ③ — ④ Setting aside time to reflect on Scripture

① — ② — ③ — ④ Praising God in song, music, prayer, or thoughts

① — ② — ③ — ④ Recognizing and responding to the Holy Spirit's guidance

① — ② — ③ — ④ Spurring your heart toward the wonder or awe of God

① — ② — ③ — ④ Expressing thankfulness to God for His goodness, gifts, and character

① — ② — ③ — ④ Forgiving others and asking them for forgiveness

① — ② — ③ — ④ Demonstrating your faith in daily life

Prayerfully reflecting on your responses, rank the top three where you most want to grow in your relationship with God?

1.

2.

3.

"The only place where we can see clearly to realign everything in our spiritual lives is in the presence of God."

What three adjustments can you make in your daily life to encourage spiritual growth in the areas you identified?

1.

2.

3.

Look up the following passages. What does each one reveal about God's presence and/or His goodness when we spend time with Him? Fill in the chart below.

PASSAGE	WHAT DOES THE PASSAGE REVEAL ABOUT GOD'S PRESENCE AND/OR HIS GOODNESS?
Psalm 16:11	
Psalm 27:4	
Psalm 34:7–9	
Psalm 84:10–12	
Psalm 91:1	

Reflecting on these passages, which ones stir your desire to connect more deeply with God? Why? In the space below, rewrite whichever passage(s) you resonate with in your own words.

In the space below, write a personal prayer asking God to spark your spiritual desire for Him and His presence every moment of every day.

LESSON TWO

We know that in God's presence there is an abundance of joy and at God's right hand are pleasures forever (Psalm 16:11), yet we live in a world where it's so easy to get distracted and become overwhelmed by everything that seems to be spiraling out of control. Our world is so noisy that we can quickly become aligned with purposes and goals other than those God has for us. That's why in the first lesson of this session, we looked at all the delights that come from being in God's presence. In this lesson, we're going to continue our self-assessment by considering what might have slipped into our lives and drawn our attention from God so we can fully realign with Him.

Throughout the Bible, an idol is anything that takes the place of God in our lives, receiving the devotion, worship, and allegiance that should be directed to Him. For the children of Israel, this occurred when they built the golden calf and worshipped it. Idols can be physical objects, desires, or anything we prioritize above God.

"The only place you can have everything realigned is when you get yourself back into the presence of God."

Look up the following passages and fill in the chart below.

PASSAGE	WHAT DOES THIS SCRIPTURE REVEAL ABOUT IDOLS AND IDOLATRY?
Exodus 20:3–5	
Psalm 115:4–8	
Jonah 2:8–9	
Romans 1:21–23	

Idols can slip into our lives and usurp God's place of priority, which is why the Easter season is so valuable for reflection and making spiritual adjustments. Prayerfully consider the following list and circle any that reveal your own idol tendencies—those areas or people receiving your devotion, allegiance, or worship other than God. What are you giving yourself to other than God—spiritually, mentally, emotionally, financially, socially, or physically?

Circle all that tempt you toward idolatry.

Money or wealth

Material possessions

Fame or recognition

Relationships or romance

Physical appearance or beauty

Social media or online presence

Politics or ideologies

Personal achievements or accomplishments

Children or family

Career or professional success

Comfort or convenience

Alcohol or drugs

Control or dominance over others

Sexual gratification

Education or knowledge

Self-idolatry or self-reliance

Other: _____

Power or status or opinions

First Corinthians 10:14 instructs us to flee from idolatry, which may mean removing something from our lives that's overtly toxic or harmful. What have you identified in your life that needs to go? Or be realigned?

I understand that sometimes what we need to adjust is not simple to do. You may not be able to quit your career or exit ministry, for example, and you certainly can't give your beloved family members away. So fleeing idolatry often means asking God for wisdom on how to put those potential idols in their rightful place, and resist turning to them for comfort, protection, or fulfillment.

Using the chart below, write down each of the phrases you circled and prayerfully develop a plan to put God in His rightful place instead.

POTENTIAL IDOL OR IDOLATRY TENDENCY	PLAN TO KEEP GOD TOP PRIORITY

Sometimes the changes we need to make in our spiritual alignment aren't what we do more or less of but where we turn when we face life's challenges. Some of the behaviors we turn to during stressful times can cause harm to ourselves or our relationships over time. Some can even become addictive.

When you're feeling overwhelmed, which of the following do you tend to turn toward for comfort? Circle all that apply.

Eating sugary food	Blaming others
Throwing yourself into work	Gossiping
Oversleeping	Over-reliance on friends
Bingeing shows	Overeating
Aggressive driving	Substance abuse
Ignoring self-care	Avoiding responsibility
Negative self-talk	Hyper-cleaning
Scrolling social media	Obsessive worrying
Shopping	Ruminating
Perfectionism	Other: _____
Excessive collecting	

🌿 Reflecting on what you circled, what are you not doing that you need to do a little more of?

🌿 What are you doing that you need to do a little less of?

🌿 What would it look like for you to turn toward God in prayer, praise, study, or simply being with Him instead of what you circled on the previous page?

In the space below, write a prayer asking God to forgive you for any idolatry you've identified, to empower you to remove any remaining idols, and to help you place your whole hope in Him.

Now just like professional athletes, to get on the playing field and run our race, we'll need to practice discipline. So, let's get focused. Let's make sure that first things are first. Let's eliminate all the things we don't want to do in order to get ourselves on that playing field and run our race and finish our course.

Read Hebrews 12:1–2.

🌿 Why is it so important to get rid of every idol and encumbrance that holds us back?

🌿 What hope does this give you as you prepare for Easter?

LESSON THREE

The most precious thing that you and I can have is the presence of God. Let me say that again: The most precious thing that you and I can have is the presence of God.

That's what the Israelites had to learn the hard way. After the golden calf incident, where God's people built their own idols, the Lord instructed Moses to pack up everything and head toward the promised land. God promised to send an angel ahead of them to drive out the many enemies that they would face. But then God delivered heartbreaking news: He would not be going with them.

Read Exodus 33:1–6.

🌿 What is God's reasoning for not accompanying His people?

🌿 How do the people respond to the news? How does their response reveal their desire for the presence of God?

Read Exodus 33:7–11.

How would you describe the relationship between Moses and God in this passage?

What parts of their relationship do you desire in your own relationship with God?

Moses pleads with God not to send them forward without His presence, emphasizing the need for God's presence as their distinguishing mark among the nations.

Read Exodus 33:12–17.

How does Moses' boldness in interceding for the people reflect his deep relationship with God?

God reassures Moses that His presence will go with them and give them rest, highlighting God's grace and mercy despite the people's sin.

What does God's promise to be with Moses and the Israelites teach us about His character?

Moses doesn't want the blessing of God without the presence of God. He doesn't want the promise of God without the presence of God. Moses and the Israelites help us recognize that even if we get all the blessings and promises of God, what's the point, if we don't have God's presence. This is the most precious thing we can have from God.

Are you pursuing the blessings of God or the God of the blessings? Mark your answer on the continuum below.

I'm pursuing the blessings of God.

I'm pursuing the God of the blessings.

Where are you clinging more to the promises of God than the God who makes the promises?

"How often do we start saying, 'God, all I want is You,' but then add, 'as long as I also get the car and the house and the spouse and the kids'?"

Where do you long for God's presence more than the promotion, more than the provision, more than the promise?

We need to be careful in our day and age, which is all about self-realization, self-actualization, self-help, everything self, self, self. We can only go so far in our own strength and in our own self without God's presence. Now, I'm not talking about the omnipresence of God that is always everywhere. I'm talking about the manifest presence of God that is with you daily and in your circumstances.

One of the greatest ways to experience God's presence is to linger with Him. That's what Joshua did as he lingered near the tent listening to Moses and God. It's something we can do as we spend time with God each day. Rather than just complete a Bible reading or lesson or prayer and rush off to the next thing, we can take time to pray to God that we want more of His presence. We can linger with God.

What does it look like for you to linger with God in prayer, study, worship, or being with Him?

Have you ever lingered with God? What did you experience?

What are three steps you can take to carve out more time to linger with God?

1.

2.

3.

The book of Hebrews emphasizes Christ's priesthood and His once-for-all sacrifice, providing believers with confident and continual access to God.

Read Hebrews 10:19–20.

🌿 What does this passage reveal about the confidence we can have to approach God, signified by the new and living way Jesus opened through His sacrifice?

🌿 What does it look like for you to draw near to God with a sincere heart and full assurance of faith?

Just as Moses sought God's presence and desired to see His glory, we are called to seek a deeper relationship with God.

Go beyond thinking about your answer here and write it out below. In what specific ways can you pursue a deeper relationship with the living God that is available because of Jesus' sacrifice?

"God always knew He would send His only begotten Son for us. The King of all kings knew He would lay down His scepter and hoist His body onto a cross to die for us."

LISA HARPER

Compassion in the Shape of the Cross

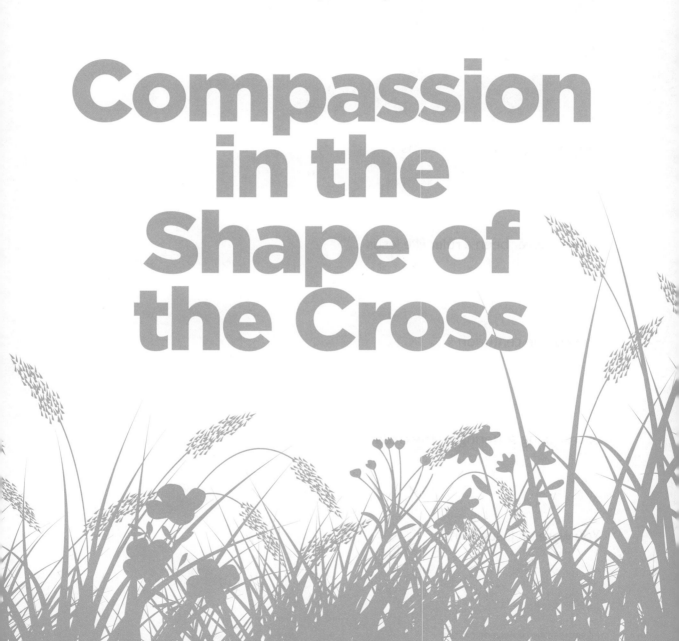

Video 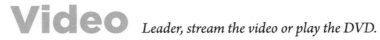 *Leader, stream the video or play the DVD.*

Each video opens with a short introduction vignette, followed by the teaching session. **As you watch, take notes on anything that stands out to you.**

> **SCRIPTURE: Revelation 17:14, 19:11–16; Mark 10:35–40, 15:33–39**

Volleyball story

King of kings and Lord of lords

There's never been a ruler like Jesus

The Roman centurion

Excruciating suffering on the cross

You were on Jesus' mind

VOCABULARY	DEFINITION
KING OF KINGS **βασιλεύς** **(basileus)**	refers to a king or ruler who has sovereign authority over a people or nation
LORD OF LORDS **κύριος** **(kyrios)**	supernatural master over all
SEPTUAGINT	the translation of the Hebrew Scriptures into the Greek
INCARNATE	Jesus is wholly God and wholly man simultaneously.
HYPOSTATIC UNION	Jesus is both divine and human at the same time.

Group Discussion

1. **Lesslie Newbigin, a theologian, says that one of the most effective lenses through which we see Jesus more clearly is each other.**

    • How have you seen or recognized Jesus more through a fellow believer, perhaps even someone doing this study with you?

    • What have other believers reminded you of during this Easter season?

2. **Invite a few volunteers to read Revelation 17:14 and 19:11–16, and then respond to the following questions.**

    • What does it mean to you that Jesus is King of kings and Lord of lords?

    • How is Jesus' authority different from any other ruler, leader, or monarch?

"He's the king of our kings. He's the Lord of all lords. And because he's completely other, there's never been a sovereign, never been an emperor, never been a ruler like Jesus. Most people didn't get it. Even his own followers didn't get it."

3. **Discuss the following.**

    • Where are you struggling to see Jesus as King of kings and Lord of lords in your life? In your relationships? In your perspectives on the world?

    • How would your life be different if you regained His perspective and truth in your life?

4. **Invite a few volunteers to read Matthew 27:27–37, and then respond to the following questions.**

   • What stood out to you from Lisa's powerful description of Jesus' death?

   • What does it reveal about Jesus that He was willing to endure so much mockery and physical abuse?

   • How does the inscription "THIS IS JESUS, THE KING OF THE JEWS" serve a dual purpose?

   • What does this passage reveal about the nature of Jesus' sacrifice?

   • In what ways does this passage deepen your understanding of Jesus' love for humanity—including you?

"Lord, help us to learn what it is to be Easter people in a Good Friday world."

5. **In the teaching, Lisa instructed you to ask the Holy Spirit to bring to the forefront of your mind a picture of someone you love, who doesn't yet know the love of Jesus—be it a parent, cousin, or coworker.**

   • Who came to your mind as you prayed?

   • Will you begin to consistently pray for them to know Jesus?

   • What opportunities have you had in the past or might have in the future to share Jesus' love with this person?

"The King of all kings saw us. When they ripped the flesh from His back, we were on His mind. When they pounded the stakes in His wrist and His heels, we were on His mind. When people spewed vulgar names, Jesus said, 'You're so worth it to me!' We have always, even at our worst, been the object of His affection."

6. **Explore these questions.**

    • What does it mean to you that you were on Jesus' mind as He endured the cross?

    • Where do you struggle to believe that you are the object of Jesus' affection?

    • How does Jesus' suffering change the way you want to live?

    • What does it look like for you to be an Easter person in a Good Friday world?

Call to Action

Leader, you will need some pieces of paper, about a quarter- or half-page for this exercise.

Pass out a piece of paper to each group member. Invite each person to write down something she needs to experience from Jesus this Easter season. Place each slip of paper into a bowl or basket, mix them up, then have each person draw one. Pray over that encounter with Christ for the remaining weeks.

Closing Prayer

Select a volunteer to read the closing prayer over the group.

Lord, You willingly gave up Your last breath before the resurrection because You think we're worth it. Lord, may we never miss the opportunity to give You thanks. Help us to understand the depths of Your sacrificial love so we can more clearly emulate You in this beautiful, broken world. In Jesus' name. Amen.

Personal Study

Don't forget to pray over an enounter
with Christ for one of your fellow group
members throughout this week.

• • •
LESSON ONE

The betrayal and arrest of Jesus highlight His unwavering commitment to God's redemptive plan and His profound love for humanity. The events of this night mark a pivotal moment that lead directly to Jesus' trial and crucifixion. In this first lesson, we're going to explore the events in the garden of Gethsemane, focusing on the betrayal by Judas Iscariot and Jesus' arrest.

Read Matthew 26:36–46.

In the space below draw a simple picture of this scene. Include depictions or names those whom Jesus chose to accompany Him into the garden.

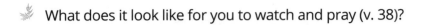 What does it look like for you to watch and pray (v. 38)?

How do these disciples respond to Jesus' request (v. 40, 43, 45)?

 *"Lord, help us see You more clearly so that we can emulate You more effectively in this beautiful, broken world."*

What deep sorrow and anguish is Jesus experiencing before His arrest?

🌿 What does this passage reveal about Jesus' relationship with the Father (v. 39 and v. 42)?

🌿 In what area of your life do you most need to declare, "Not my will, but yours be done"?

Judas was one of the twelve disciples who had walked and talked and traveled with Jesus. He'd sat under Jesus' powerful teaching, watched His incredible miracles, and experienced the depths of Jesus' kindness and compassion. Yet Judas arrives with an armed crowd to arrest Jesus. He then betrays Jesus with a kiss, a gesture that usually symbolizes affection, acceptance, and respect. Jesus responds with calm authority, even as one of His companions reacts with violence.

Read Matthew 26:47–56 and Psalm 41:9.

 How do Judas' actions fulfill the prophecy of the psalm?

 What does Jesus' response to the person who draws a sword (identified as Peter in John 18:10) reveal about Jesus' authority and character?

 What does Jesus' response teach us about handling conflict?

"I think it behooves us to spend just a few minutes—as heavy as it is—in the historical reality of what it meant for incarnate Jesus to be crucified."

What does Jesus' declaration about the angels that can be sent reveal about His authority and power?

How does the disciples deserting Jesus fulfill the prophecy of Zechariah 13:7?

What does it reveal about Jesus' love for you that He could have stopped these events at any time and yet willingly endured them?

The events in the garden of Gethsemane, as well as Judas' betrayal and the disciples running away, challenge us to reflect on our own faithfulness to Jesus, the importance of staying vigilant in prayer, and relying on God rather than ourselves in difficult times. But as we'll see in Lesson Two, the trials that Jesus will face will only continue to intensify.

LESSON TWO

After His arrest, Jesus is taken before Caiaphas, the high priest, and the Sanhedrin—the Jewish ruling council. The encounter highlights the intense tension between Jesus and the religious authorities that has been building throughout His ministry. From the start, Jesus had been a threat to their systems and power. Now the religious leaders gather false witnesses to justify putting Jesus to death.

Read Matthew 26:57–67.

What are three elements that stand out to you about those accusing Jesus and Jesus' response?

1.

2.

3.

Despite the injustice and false accusations, Jesus remains faithful and reveals Himself as the Messiah. Soon, the chief priests and the elders who want Jesus executed take Him to their Roman governor, Pontius Pilate. Both trials are steeped in prophetic fulfillment, highlighting that Jesus' suffering was foretold and part of God's redemptive plan.

Read Matthew 27:11–26.

What are three elements that stand out to you about those accusing Jesus and Jesus' response?

1.

2.

3.

"Remember, Jesus didn't absolve himself from pain. He's perfectly incarnate. That means He is completely God, transcendent, wholly other, and perfectly man simultaneously. This is one of the greatest truths of our faith."

In both trials, Jesus gives the same response to the false accusations. Fill in the chart below noting the response of Jesus and how this fulfills prophecy.

QUESTION	BIBLE PASSAGE	ANSWER
In the face of false accusations, what response does Jesus give at both trials?	Matthew 26:62–63 Matthew 27:12	
How does Jesus' response to the false accusations fulfill Old Testament prophecy?	Isaiah 53:7	

The high priest reacts to Jesus' declaration by tearing his clothes, a sign of outrage, and accuses Jesus of blasphemy. The council agrees that Jesus deserves death. This reaction reveals their inability to recognize Jesus as the Messiah and their rigid adherence to their interpretations of the law.

In both trials, both the Sanhedrin and Pilate question Jesus about His identity. Fill in the chart below noting the response of Jesus and how this fulfills prophecy.

QUESTION	BIBLE PASSAGE	ANSWER
What does Jesus' answer to the high priest at the Sanhedrin reveal about His identity?	Matthew 26:53–64	
How does Jesus' response fulfill Old Testament prophecy?	Daniel 7:13–14	
What does Jesus' answer to Pilate reveal about His identity?	Matthew 27:11	
How is Jesus more than just King of one people group according to Old Testament prophecy?	Isaiah 9:6–7	

Pilate knows the religious leaders brought Jesus to him out of jealousy and their own selfish desires. His wife even warns him about a disturbing dream about Jesus and declares him innocent (v. 19). Pilate releases Jesus, but the crowds controlled by the religious leaders demand the release of Barabbas, a guilty prisoner, over innocent Jesus. Barabbas goes free and Jesus is beaten before He will make the ultimate sacrifice on the cross.

Read Isaiah 53.

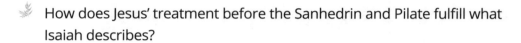 How does Jesus' treatment before the Sanhedrin and Pilate fulfill what Isaiah describes?

How do these events deepen your understanding of Jesus' sacrifice?

• • •

LESSON THREE

After Jesus stood trial before Pilate, He was taken to the Praetorium, which was the Roman governor's residence. Sometimes it's hard to wrap our heads and hearts—our minds and emotions—around all that Jesus endured as He faced the cross. Matthew 27:27–31 offers a detailed account of the mockery and violence that Jesus endured at the hands of Roman soldiers.

Read the following passage and underline any descriptions of Jesus' suffering.

Then the governor's soldiers took Jesus into the Praetorium and gathered the whole company of soldiers around him. They stripped him and put a scarlet robe on him, and then twisted together a crown of thorns and set it on his head. They put a staff in his right hand. Then they knelt in front of him and mocked him. "Hail, king of the Jews!" they said. They spit on him, and took the staff and struck him on the head again and again. After they had mocked him, they took off the robe and put his own clothes on him. Then they led him away to crucify him.

As they were going out, they met a man from Cyrene, named Simon, and they forced him to carry the cross. They came to a place called Golgotha (which means "the place of the skull"). There they offered Jesus wine to drink, mixed with gall; but after tasting it, he refused to drink it. When they had crucified him, they divided up his clothes by casting lots. And sitting down, they kept watch over him there. Above his head they placed the written charge against him: THIS IS JESUS, KING OF THE JEWS.

Matthew 27:27–37 (NIV)

What do the soldiers' actions reveal about human nature and the corruption of earthly power?

 *"Roman scourging was a terrifying punishment. The delinquent was stripped, bound to a post or pillar, or sometimes simply thrown to the ground. No minimum number of strokes was prescribed by Roman law, and men condemned to flagellation frequently collapsed and died from the flogging."*

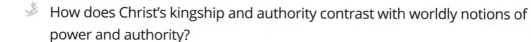

 How does Christ's kingship and authority contrast with worldly notions of power and authority?

Through the soldiers' behavior, we see the fulfillment of prophecy and the profound reality of Jesus as the suffering servant and true king. Reflecting on these events challenges us to appreciate more deeply the cost of our redemption and to live in a way that honors His sacrifice.

How does reflecting on the suffering Jesus endured for our salvation deepen your gratitude toward Him? In the space below, write a prayer of thanks for what Jesus sacrificed for you.

From noon until three in the afternoon, a sudden darkness overcomes the land, despite it being midday. Jesus cries out to God in anguish, emphasizing the depths of the agony and alienation as He endures the cross and carries the sin of the world. Those within earshot misunderstand Jesus' cry, thinking He is calling for Elijah. One person offers him wine vinegar to drink, while others watch wondering what will happen next. With a final loud cry, Jesus surrenders His spirit and dies.

Read Matthew 27:45–56.

In verses 51-53, eight supernatural events take place immediately following Jesus' death. Fill in the chart below using these three verses.

VERSE	WHAT SUPERNATURAL EVENTS FOLLOWED JESUS' DEATH?
Matthew 27:51 (3 things happen)	
Matthew 27:52 (2 things happen)	
Matthew 27:53 (3 things happen)	

How do these supernatural events demonstrate the power of Jesus' death and foreshadow Jesus' victory over death?

How does the presence of faithful women underscore their importance in Jesus' life and ministry? How can you emulate their devotion to Christ?

What are three practical ways you can boldly and fearlessly declare Jesus as Lord in your daily life?

1.

2.

3.

"Jesus has commissioned us to come and see for ourselves, and then go into a lost and broken world and declare loudly that He is alive."

CHRISTINE CAINE

Come and See, Go and Tell

Video 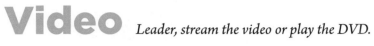 *Leader, stream the video or play the DVD.*

Each video opens with a short introduction vignette, followed by the teaching session. **As you watch, take notes on anything that stands out to you.**

> **SCRIPTURE: Matthew 28:1–10; 1 Corinthians 15:12–19**

Mary, a common name

Supernatural components of faith

Come and see

Go and tell

Jesus valued, dignified, and esteemed women

The great commissioning

Group Discussion

"The death of Jesus happens on Friday, which is often called Good Friday, and then there's silent Saturday. It's a day of wondering what has happened and what is going on. So many of us live in that in-between place where perhaps the dream has died, the promise has died, the opportunity has died. The Easter message does not finish on Saturday. There's always a resurrection Sunday. This is what sets our faith apart."

1. **Discuss the following.**

   • Where are you facing a "silent Saturday" and perhaps wrestling with the death of a dream, promise, or opportunity?

   • How have you encountered God in this season?

   • What are you discovering about His presence and character?

   • What hope do you find in Jesus' resurrection that He can make all things new?

2. **Invite a few volunteers to read Matthew 28:1–7, and then respond to the following questions.**

   • What miraculous events surrounded the women's arrival at the tomb?

   • How do the women respond?

   • How do you respond to the powerful works of God in your life?

   • How can you pursue Jesus in your daily life, especially in times of hardship or uncertainty, with devotion similar to the women who came to the tomb?

"There are four verbs that the angel of the Lord says to the women: come *and* see *and* go *and* tell *(Matthew 28:6–7). This is what happens when you encounter a resurrected Savior."*

3. **Consider the following.**

- What does it mean to you that Jesus invites you to come and see Him?

- Sometimes it's tempting to believe that you need to clean yourself up or get yourself together before you come to Jesus. Where do you struggle with this kind of thinking?

- Where have you seen Jesus' presence or work in your life?

- After you answer the call to come and see Jesus, why should you go and tell others about what you've encountered?

- Of the four verbs, which do you struggle with the most? Which comes most easily? Explain.

"Jesus came to make us dangerous to the kingdom of darkness, that we would proclaim His good news to a lost and broken world."

4. **Invite a few volunteers to read 1 Corinthians 15:12–19, and then respond to the following questions.**

- Why is Christ's resurrection the linchpin of the Christian life?

- What is possible apart from the resurrection?

- How does the reality of Jesus' victory over death influence your daily actions, decisions, and overall perspective on life?

> *"Jesus always valued, included, esteemed, and empowered women. So, He says, 'Go and tell the men that I have risen, just as I have said.' And commissioning is what we have all been called to do—to go into all the world and make disciples."*

5. **Explore the following questions.**

- How should the message of the resurrection, as experienced by the women, affect the lives of believers today?

- What does the role of the women as the first witnesses to the resurrection tell us about God's values and the nature of His kingdom?

- What does it look like for you to declare the good news of Jesus' resurrection in your everyday life?

- What holds you back from sharing the good news of Jesus with others?

- How can you become a cheerleader for other people who are sharing the good news of Jesus and making disciples?

6. **Discuss the following.**

    • What has been most meaningful for you during this season of Easter thus far?

    • How has your heart been prepared for the resurrection of the Christ?

    • How has this Easter season made you more expectant for Jesus to unleash His power and fulfill His promises in your life?

Call to Action

Leader, you will need some pieces of paper, about a quarter- or half-page for this exercise.

Pass out pieces of paper to each group member. Invite each person to write down what they're most grateful for during this Easter season. Place each slip of paper into a bowl or basket, mix them up, and then have each person draw one and read the words aloud as a prayer of thanks.

Closing Prayer

Select a volunteer to read the closing prayer over the group.

Lord Jesus, thank You for this incredible season where we live as Easter people every day. Help us to come and see, and go and tell the good news You've given to us with boldness. We are so thankful for You. We love You. In Jesus' name. Amen.

Personal Study

Don't forget to pray for a continued posture of gratitude during this Easter season for one of your fellow group members throughout this week.

• • •
LESSON ONE

On the morning of the resurrection, we must remember that Jesus had been betrayed by Judas, forsaken by His disciples, denied by Peter, tried by the Sanhedrin, condemned to die by Pilate, crucified at Calvary, and buried in the tomb of Joseph. Jesus was dead.

The Gospel of Matthew tells us that Mary Magdalene and the other Mary— presumably the mother of James and Joseph—went to view the tomb at dawn after the Sabbath. They were stunned when they arrived because they saw that the tomb was open, the stone was rolled away, an angel of the Lord was sitting on this very stone, His clothing was as white as snow, and the guards were like dead men paralyzed with fear. No wonder the women were in shock because this is not what anyone in the history of the world expects to see when they arrive at a burial site.

No wonder the angel of the Lord said to them, "Don't be afraid." I'm surprised that the women had not passed out at this point! The angel of the Lord went on to say that he knew the women were looking for Jesus, who had been crucified, and informed them that Jesus was no longer there because He had risen, just as He said He would. From my perspective, this visitation is not going how anyone had planned at this point.

Then the angel instructed the women to, "Come and see the place where he lay. Then go quickly and tell his disciples" (Matthew 28:6–7). It all begins with the word *come*. The word *come* is a welcoming word. It's an invitation word, an embracing word.

Look up the following passages. What does each one offer as an invitation to come? Fill in the chart below.

PASSAGE	WHAT IS THE INVITATION TO *COME*?
Matthew 4:19	
Matthew 11:28	
Matthew 19:14	
Revelation 22:17	

The invitation to come to the resurrected Jesus is extended to us all.

You can come to the one who offers forgiveness, salvation, peace, hope, and power to all who believe in him. You don't have to follow a special set of rules to come to Jesus. You don't have to be born into a special family to come to Jesus. You don't have to be raised in church to come to Jesus. You don't have to have lived a perfect life to come to Jesus. You don't have to know the right people to come to Jesus. You don't have to behave a certain way to come to Jesus.

You don't have to dress a particular way to come to Jesus. You don't have to possess a certain talent or gift to come to Jesus. You don't need to belong to a certain socio-economic demographic to come to Jesus. You don't have to go to the right school to come to Jesus. You don't have to live in the right neighborhood to come to Jesus. You don't need to be a certain ethnicity, age, or gender to come to Jesus. Anyone can come to Jesus. Now that, my friend, is good news.

I (Christine) want to pause and take a moment right now to ask you if you have come to Jesus.

Yes   *No*   **I am not asking if you go to church, or if you go to Bible study, or if you were raised in a Christian home, or if you have Christian friends. I am asking if you have come to Jesus for yourself? Circle your response.**

Yes   *No*   **Have you encountered the resurrected Jesus for yourself? Circle your response.**

If you have not, then I want to give you the opportunity right at this moment in this study to open your heart and receive the love, grace, forgiveness, and mercy of God that is available to you.

You do not need to spend one more moment wondering if He would invite, accept, or welcome you. You can come to Jesus right now, right as you are, wherever you are. Do not delay for one moment because only Jesus Christ offers us forgiveness for our past, a brand-new life for today, and a hope for the future.

Yes   **No**   **Would you come to Jesus today?**
Circle your response.

You can bring your burdens to Jesus today. You can bring your disappointments to Jesus today. You can bring your hurts to Jesus today. You can bring your questions to Jesus today. You can bring your doubts to Jesus today. He is alive and not dead. He can handle it all. His shoulders are broad enough to carry it all. He loves you so. He sees. He knows. He cares.

After instructing the women to come, the angel instructs them to see.

Reread Matthew 28:6–7.

What did the angel invite the women to see?

🌿 Why was this so important for their faith?

🌿 Describe a time when you saw or encountered Jesus or His presence in a way that transformed you.

After instructing the women to come and see, the angel instructs them to go. Later in the same chapter, Jesus delivers the Great Commission.

Read Matthew 28:19–20.

🌿 What does Jesus' command to "go" reveal about your role in sharing the good news of Jesus?

 How does Jesus' command to "go" imply active and intentional movement rather than passive waiting?

> *"Jesus defeated hell. He defeated death. He has given us a life beyond our past, a life beyond our sin."*

When it comes to sharing the gospel, do you tend to be someone who passively holds back or who actively moves forward? Circle one.

I tend to passively wait for opportunities to share the gospel.

I tend to actively move toward opportunities to share the gospel.

After instructing the women to come, see, and go, the angel instructs them to tell.

Which of the following do you struggle with when it comes to telling others about your faith? Circle all that apply.

Fear of rejection	Feeling inexperienced
Lack of knowledge	Feeling inadequate
Negative past experiences	Afraid of alienating others
Fear of criticism	Doubting abilities
Lack of confidence	Not wanting to seem disrespectful
Uncertainty about the response	Other: _____

Sometimes telling others about your faith can be challenging. Yet it remains a fundamental aspect of the Christian walk—and the good news is that you don't have to do it alone.

Read Acts 1:8.

 Who can you rely on to help you as you tell others about Jesus?

Read Philippians 1:6.

 How will sharing your faith deepen your understanding of Christ?

Read 2 Timothy 4:2.

What are three practical ways you can be ready in season and out of season to tell others about Jesus.

1.

2.

3.

By recalling these Scriptures and the power of the Holy Spirit, we can tell others about Jesus. Let us commit to being bold, prepared, and gracious as we share our hope in the resurrected Christ with the world.

LESSON TWO

The first people Jesus told to take the gospel into the world were women. Now, under the Roman Empire in which Jesus lived, a woman was not a credible witness in a court of law. And yet Jesus entrusts the news of His resurrection to them. He puts all the chips in one basket, by sending two women to go and tell the disciples. While Jesus' choice likely stunned many people, it was consistent with His character and the way He treated others throughout His earthly ministry. To those who were told, "You're out!" Jesus declared, "You're in!" To those who were on the margins, Jesus brought them into the center of work and life. To those who were excluded, Jesus went out of His way to include. And women were no exception!

Read Luke 8:1–3.

Which women are listed in this passage and what role did they play in Jesus' ministry? Fill in the chart below.

WOMEN'S NAMES	ROLE IN JESUS' MINISTRY

Read Luke 24:10.

Which women are listed in this passage and what role did they play in Jesus' ministry? Circle the names that are mentioned in both passages.

WOMEN'S NAMES	ROLE IN JESUS' MINISTRY

How do these passages reveal the integral role of women in sustaining and promoting Jesus' mission?

 What does it mean to you personally that Jesus would entrust the greatest news of all time—His resurrection—to women?

"Right from the first second of the resurrection, Jesus is saying, 'Oh you're included in my mission. You're included in my work. I'm entrusting the most important news to you!'"

How does this challenge you to be more active and bolder in sharing the news of Jesus?

Women have played vital roles in the ministry of Jesus and mission of the church from its inception. The New Testament highlights several women who were instrumental in spreading the gospel and helping the early church flourish. Fill in the following chart on the right.

What can you learn to expect when defined by Jesus as those who are sharing the good news of Jesus who are not...

PASSAGE	NAME OF WOMAN	DETAILS
Acts 16:14–15		Description of her: Impact on early church:
Romans 16:1–2		Description of her: Impact on early church:
Acts 18:24–26		Description of her: Impact on early church:

🌿 What steps can you take to ensure the diverse gifts and callings of women, who are sharing the good news of Jesus with others, are recognized, valued, and celebrated?

🌿 Does anything hold you back from recognizing yourself as someone who has been called and gifted to share the good news of Jesus? If so, how can you move beyond it?

· · ·
LESSON THREE

Easter invites us into a time of celebration of the death and resurrection of Jesus, but it also reminds us of the incredible opportunity available to us all. The resurrection empowers us to live a new life in Christ. It signifies a transformation from the old self to becoming a new creation in Christ (2 Corinthians 5:17).

Read Romans 6:4.

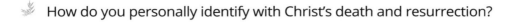 How do you personally identify with Christ's death and resurrection?

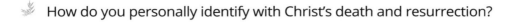 What old habits or behaviors do you still need to bury as you embrace your new life in Christ?

What are three things you can do to walk in the newness of life available through Christ's resurrection each day?

1.

2.

3.

How has this Easter season challenged you to remain vigilant and attentive to Christ's presence and work in your life?

How has this Easter season made you more expectant for Jesus to show up in power and fulfill His promises in your life?

"Our job is to make Jesus' last command our first priority."

How do you feel about Easter now that you have completed this study? Circle any that apply.

Grateful	Empowered	Humbled
Challenged	Transformed	Joyful
Hopeful	Equipped	Other: _____

How has your relationship with God and others changed during this study?

+ Relationship changed with God:

+ Relationship changed with others:

What's your greatest takeaway from this study?

Stations of
the Cross

The Stations of the Cross are a series of images of Jesus' journey of suffering. Celebrated by Roman Catholic believers for centuries, the Stations of the Cross are utilized as a tool to appreciate Jesus' sacrifice before Easter. The traditional stations represent fourteen possible crucial moments in the trial, crucifixion, and burial of Jesus.

On Good Friday, 1991, Pope John Paul II introduced a new form of devotions called *The Scriptural Way of the Cross* to reflect more deeply on the scriptural accounts, and less on the church's traditional imagery. Since then, different passages and meditations have been released most years.

Jesus in the
Garden of Gethsemane

MATTHEW 26:36–41

1

Jesus is betrayed
by Judas and arrested

MARK 14:43-46

2

Jesus is condemned
by the Sanhedrin

LUKE 22:66–71

3

Jesus takes up
His cross

JOHN 19:6, 15–17

7

Jesus is helped by
Simon to carry His cross

MARK 15:21

8

Jesus meets the
women of Jerusalem

LUKE 23:27–31

9

Stations of the Cross

Taken from: https://www.usccb.org/prayers/scriptural-stations-cross

Pope John II added a fifteenth station on resurrection:
https://friendsofcama.blogspot.com/2011/06/15th-station-of-cross-resurrection.html

Jesus dies
on the cross

LUKE 23:44–46

13

Jesus is
denied by Peter

MATTHEW 26:69–75

4

Jesus is
judged by Pilate

MARK 15:1–5, 15

5

Jesus is scourged and
crowned with thorns

JOHN 19:1–3

6

Jesus
is crucified

LUKE 23:33–34

10

Jesus promises His
kingdom to the good thief

LUKE 23:39–43

11

Jesus speaks to Mary
and the disciples

JOHN 19:25–27

12

Jesus is placed
in the tomb

MATTHEW 27:57–60

14

Additional interesting perspectives:
https://www.catholicmom.com/articles/2011/04/04/the-scriptural-way-of-the-cross

Leader's Guide

Thank you for your willingness to lead your group through *The Promise and Power of Easter: Captivated by the Cross and Resurrection of Jesus*. The rewards of leading are different from the rewards of participating, and we hope you find your own walk with Jesus deepened by this experience. This leader's guide will give you some tips on how to prepare for your time together and facilitate a meaningful experience for your group members.

WHAT DOES IT TAKE TO LEAD THIS STUDY?

Get together and watch God show up. Seriously, that's the basics of how a small group works. Gather several people together who have a hunger for God, want to learn more about what is in store for them at "the renewal of all things" (Matthew 19:28), and are willing to be open and honest with God and themselves. You don't have to be a pastor, priest, theologian, or counselor to lead a group through this study. Just invite people over, watch the video, and talk about it. All you need is a willing heart, a little courage, and God will do the rest. Really.

HOW THIS STUDY WORKS

There are two important pieces to *The Promise and Power of Easter* small-group study: (1) the four-session video teaching and (2) this study guide. Make sure everyone in your group has a copy of the study guide. The great part is that each study guide includes free access to streaming all of the video teaching.

Each video session is approximately twenty-four minutes in length. There is a short introduction vignette with both Chris and Lisa before each teaching session. When your group meets together, you will watch the video and discuss the session. This study is perfect for home groups, classroom settings, Sunday school classes, and any variety of large- or small-group gatherings—though you may need to modify the discussion time depending on the size of the class. Whether you meet weekly, biweekly, watch the videos as a group, watch the videos individually and gather for discussion, or any other format that fits your context, the goal is to share this teaching from Lisa and Chris with others in lively, provocative, and edifying discussions.

A FEW TIPS FOR LEADING A GROUP

The setting really matters. Select an environment that's conducive to people relaxing and getting real. Remember, the Enemy likes to distract us when it comes to seeking closeness to God in any way, so do what you can to remove these obstacles from your group (silence cell phones, limit background noise, no texting).

Have some refreshments! Coffee and water will do; cookies and snacks are even better. People tend to be nervous when they join a new group, so if you can give them something to hold on to (like a warm mug of coffee), they will relax a lot more. It's human nature.

Good equipment is important. Meet where you can watch the video sessions on a screen big enough for everyone to see and enjoy. Get or borrow the best gear you can. Also, *be sure to test your media equipment ahead of time to make sure everything is in working condition*. This way, if something isn't working, you can fix it or make other arrangements before the meeting begins. (You'll be amazed at how the Enemy will try to mess things up for you!)

Be honest. Remember that your honesty will set the tone for your time together. Be willing to answer questions personally, as this will set the pace for the length of your group members' responses and will make others more comfortable in sharing.

Stick to the schedule. Strive to begin and end at the same time each week. The people in your group are busy, and if they can trust you to be a good steward of their time, they will be more willing to come back each week. Of course, you want to be open to the work God is doing in the group members as they are challenged to reconsider some of their preconceived ideas about Easter and this time leading up to Christ's resurrection. At times you may want to linger in discussion. Remember, the clock serves you; your group doesn't serve the clock. But work to respect the group's time, especially when it comes to limiting the discussion times.

Don't be afraid of silence or emotion. Welcome awkward moments. The material presented during this study will likely challenge the group members to consider some personal emotions or experiences they have not connected to the season of Easter.

Don't dominate the conversation. Even though you are the leader, you are also a member of this small group. So don't steamroll over others in an attempt to lead—and don't let anyone else in the group do so either.

Prepare for your meeting. Watch the video for the meeting ahead of time. Though it may feel a bit like cheating because you'll know what's coming, you'll be better prepared for what the session might stir in the hearts of your group members. Also review all discussion questions so you are fully prepared for where the conversation may go. Trust the Holy Spirit in guiding you and the discussion time. The most important thing you can do is simply pray ahead of time each week:

> *Lord Jesus, come and rule this time. Let Your Spirit fill this place. Bring Your kingdom here. Take us right to the things we really need to talk about and rescue us from every distraction. Show us Your heart, Father. Meet each of us here. Give us Your grace and love for one another as we learn and grow in anticipation of Your coming here to live with all of us. Thank You in advance. In Your name I pray.*

Make sure your group members are prepared. A week or two before the first meeting, send out an email with a reminder to purchase a study guide (available at all online retail sites). Or, secure enough copies for your entire group to hand out at your first gathering. Send out a reminder email or a text a couple of days before the meeting to make sure people don't forget when and where you are meeting.

AS YOU GATHER

You will find the following counsel to be especially helpful when you meet for the first time as a group. We offer these comments in the spirit of "here is what we would do if we were leading a group through this study."

First, as the group gathers, start your time with introductions if people don't know each other. Begin with yourself and share your name, how long you've been a follower of Christ, if you have a spouse and/or children, and what you want to learn most about *The Promise and Power of Easter*. Going first will put the group more at ease.

After each person has introduced themselves, share—in no more than five minutes—what your hopes are for the group. Then jump right into watching the video session, as this will help get things started on a strong note. In the following weeks you will then want to start by allowing folks to catch up a little—say, five minutes or so. Too much of this burns up your meeting time, but you have to allow some room for it because it helps build relationships among the group members.

Note that each group will have its own personality and dynamics. Typically, people will hold back the first week or two until they feel the group is safe. Then they will begin to share. Again, don't let it throw you if your group seems a bit awkward at first. Of course, some people never want to talk, so you'll need to coax them out as time goes on. But let it go the first week.

INSIGHT FOR DISCUSSION

If the group members are in any way open to talking about their lives as it relates to this material, you will not have enough time for every question suggested in this study guide. That's okay! Pick the questions ahead of time that you know you want to cover, just in case you end up only having time to discuss a few of them.

You set the tone for the group. Your honesty and vulnerability during discussion times will tell them what they can share. How long you talk will give them an example of how long they should. So give some thought to what stories or insights from your own work in the study guide you want to highlight.

WARNING: The greatest temptation for most small-group leaders is to add to the video teaching with a little "teaching session" of their own. This is unhelpful for two reasons:

1. The discussion time will be the richest time during your meeting. The video sessions are the teaching. If you add to the teaching, you sacrifice precious time for discussion and can distract from the intended teaching.

2. You don't want your group members teaching, lecturing, or correcting one another. Every person is at a different place in his or her spiritual journey, and that's good. The best way to encourage productive discussion after a teaching is to begin the conversation straight away with whichever question in this guide you selected to begin with.

A STRONG CLOSE

Some of the best learning times will take place after the group time as God brings new insights to the participants during the week. Encourage group members to write down any questions they have as they do the Bible study work in between group meetings. Make sure they know you are available for them. Take advantage of the activity at the close of each session and encourage group members to pray for the member's request they receive. End your meeting time following either the prompted prayer or having a volunteer pray over your group, and respect this as the official close of your meeting time. This helps establish a set ending and indicates to everyone they are good to go!

Thank you again for taking the time to lead your group. May God reward your efforts and dedication and make your time together in *The Promise and Power of Easter* a revival of being utterly captivated by the cross and resurrection of Jesus!

About the Authors

MEET CHRISTINE CAINE

Christine Caine is a speaker, activist, and bestselling author. She and her husband, Nick, founded The A21 Campaign, an anti–human trafficking organization. They also founded Propel Women, an initiative that is dedicated to coming alongside women all over the globe to activate their God-given purpose. You can tune into Christine's weekly podcast, *Equip & Empower*, or her TBN television program to be encouraged with the hope of Jesus wherever you are. To learn more about Christine, visit www.christinecaine.com.

MEET LISA HARPER

Lauded as a "hilarious storyteller" and "theological storyteller," Lisa Harper is anything but stereotypical! She is known for emphasizing that accruing knowledge about God pales next to a real and intimate relationship with Jesus. Lisa has 30+ years of church and para-church ministry leadership, as well as a decade speaking on-tour with Women of Faith. She holds a Master of Theological Studies from Covenant Seminary and is in the thesis stage of an earned doctorate at Denver Seminary. She is a regular on TBN's globally syndicated *Better Together* show and has published multiple books and Bible studies. Lisa has also been leading the same weekly Bible study in her neighborhood for fifteen years. The most noticeable thing about Lisa Harper is her authenticity and love for Christ. But her greatest accomplishment to date is getting to become Missy's mom through the miracle of adoption in 2014!

Scripture
Cutout Artwork

Oh, Lord God

How am I
to know?

GENESIS 15:8

I WILL NEVER
leave you
or forsake you.

Deuteronomy 31:8

And the curtain was

torn in two, from top to bottom.

MARK 15:38

DO NOT
be afraid.
Go and tell.

Matthew 28:10

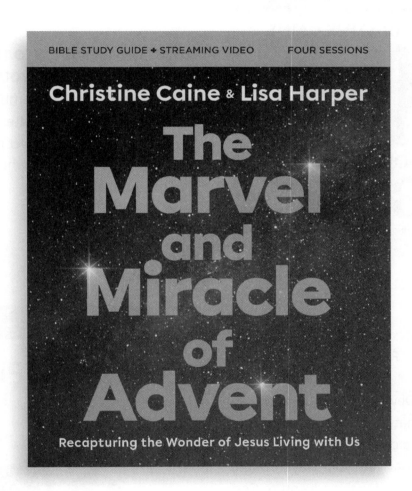

Also Available From Christine

MOVE CONFIDENTLY INTO THE PURPOSE GOD HAS FOR YOU
With a rallying cry to "remember Lot's wife," Christine motivates us to stop looking back, to let go, and to move forward into what God promises for our lives.

FAITH THAT CANNOT BE SHAKEN IS POSSIBLE
Develop a relentless faith so that the next time life throws you a curveball, you will be able to navigate your way through, still living the adventure God planned for you!

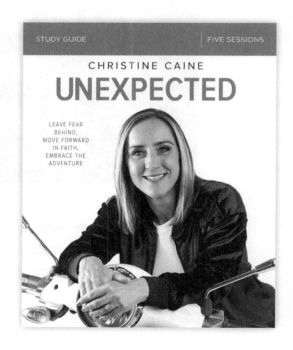

Also Available From Christine

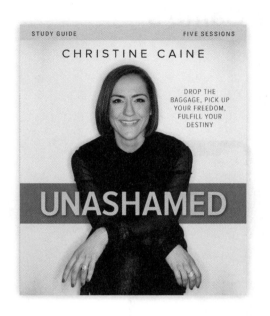

**TODAY IS THE DAY
TO FULFILL YOUR DESTINY**
Christine teaches you a way out of
shame by helping you rediscover
the power of God to overcome
our mistakes, our inadequacies,
our pasts, and our limitations.

**DARE TO DO WHAT
GOD CALLS YOU TO**
Learn from Christine
life-transforming insights
about how to overcome
the challenges and often
painful circumstances we all
experience, and to use those
experiences to be a catalyst
for change—in ourselves and
those around us.

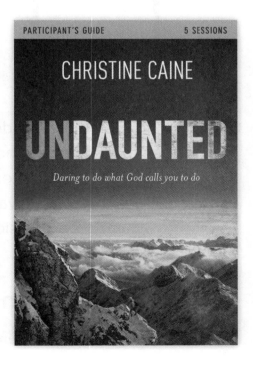

Discover your God-given purpose with Christine Caine's inspiring podcasts

New episodes every Monday and Thursday.

On her Equip & Empower podcast, Christine shares insights on navigating challenges and embracing your God-given potential, while Life & Leadership offers practical conversations that will activate you in your personal and professional life.

Streaming on all platforms

Learn more at ChristineCaine.com/Podcast

OUR MISSION IS TO END SLAVERY

But we can't do it without you.

A21 is committed to ending human trafficking by fighting to protect vulnerable people, recover victims, and empower survivors. Together, we can create lasting change and a world where everyone is free.

Learn more about A21 at A21.org

Have You Heard Lisa Harper's Podcast?

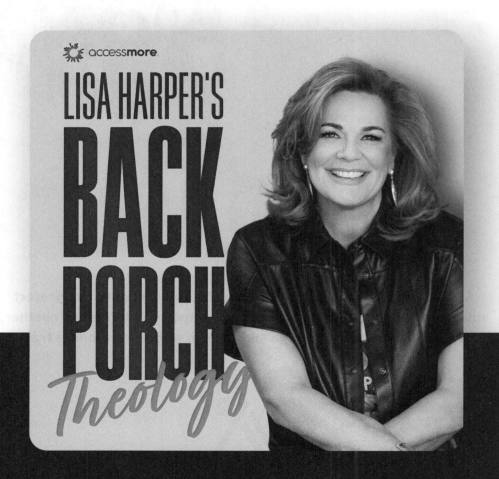

LISTEN NOW ON ✹ access**more**.

Also Available From Lisa

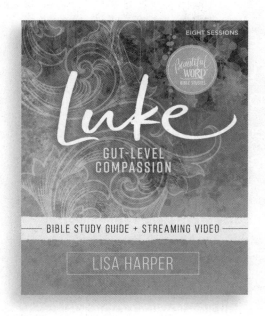

PERFECTION NOT REQUIRED
In this eight-session study, Lisa teaches the gospel that doesn't celebrate the elite, but embraces the outliers, outcasts, and overlooked!

RISKING EVERYTHING IS SO WORTH IT
In this eight-session study, Lisa reveals how the Holy Spirit catapults believers forward with power, grace, and authority to dramatically impact the world.

Join us for the

KERYGMA
Summit

K

lean *in*. learn. LAUNCH.

THE KERYGMA SUMMIT IS A CAREFULLY CURATED, 3-DAY ACCREDITED PROGRAM taught by engaging professors, theological scholars, and ministry leaders to better equip women in areas of sound biblical exegesis, hermeneutics, and practical theology.

It's like a boot camp for Bible-loving chicks! Laughter is on the agenda because while the content is substantive the atmosphere is anything but stuffy - we can almost guarantee you'll establish real friendships with thousands of other ministry leaders from all over the world!

May 1-3, 2025 & April 23-25, 2026

TO LEARN MORE, VISIT WWW.KERYGMASUMMIT.COM

FOUND
COLLECTIVE

For every age and stage of life, Found Collective
is a brand new multigenerational gathering
of women who are leaning into Jesus.

**To stay up to date on all things
Found Collective, text FOUND to 21947**